Cumbria Buses: Barrow in Furness 1948 to 1989

1948 to 1989

Stuart Emmett

Text © Stuart Emmett, 2020.
First published in the United Kingdom, 2020,
by Stenlake Publishing Ltd.,
54-58 Mill Square, Catrine,
Ayrshire, KA5 6RD

Telephone: 01290 551122
www.stenlake.co.uk

ISBN 9781840338614

Printed by P2D,
1 Newlands Road,
Westoning,
MK45 5LD

**The publishers regret that they cannot supply
copies of any pictures featured in this book.**

Picture Acknowledgements

Unless stated below, the pictures are from my own collection that is made up of our family pictures and other sources. For the latter, where the original photographer cannot be traced, I offer my apologies to them for the lack of accreditation and would be pleased to be able to correct this in future editions.

John Cockshott Archive from The Transport Library: page 22.

Omnibus Society Archive: page 3 (left).

PM Photography: page 30.

Travel Lens Photographic: pages 9, 20, 28 (upper), 29, 35, 38 (upper).

Ron Wellings from The Transport Library: page 28 (lower).

Graham Hill PRV.org.uk: pages 17, 27, 32 (left).

Sources

Ian L. Cormack, *Seventy-Five Years on Wheels*, self-published, 1960.

Ian L. Cormack, *Ninety Years on Wheels*, self-published, 1973.

Ian L. Cormack, *Barrow-in-Furness Transport*, self-published, 1977.

Barrow/Darlington/Hartlepool's Fleet History, PA15 from PSVC/OS, 1984.

Harry Postlewaite, *Transport in Barrow in Furness*, Venture Publications, 2013.

Mike Eyre, Classic Bus, April/May 2019.

Introduction

As a young teenager in late July 1961 I went to stay with my Granddad in Barrow for three weeks. He lived on Beach Crescent a small strip of land 11 miles long and mainly less than 1 mile across which shelters Barrow from the direct impacts of the we Barrow then had a population of around 70,000, with nearly 10,000 of them living on the largely residential Walney Islar ... ... the part called Vickerstown, named after the Vickers shipyard). In 1961 Barrow was dominated by the large and extensive Vickers Armstrong Shipyard on Barrow Island which was originally created by lock gates to allow access into the Irish Sea. Barrow Island is, therefore, a manmade island, sandwiched between Walney Island and the mainland and joined by the 315 metre long High Level Bridge, (also called the Michaelson Bridge).

Barrow 112 on Walney Promenade ready to turn down Ocean Road with the shipyard and slipways on Barrow Island in the background across the Walney Channel. From Walney Promenade I saw British Prestige, *a tanker for BP, launched on the 28th July 1961. The previous year I saw HMS* Dreadnought, *a Navy nuclear submarine being launched.*

Barrow 149 at the top of Beech Crescent on Walney Island. Having dropped off its last passengers it will turn right for the Biggar Bank terminus. The shipyard cranes can be seen in the background and these, along with the town hall and the ironworks, monopolised the Barrow skyline in 1961.

Bus Routes in 1961

Barrow is relatively flat and many of the shipyard workers cycled to and from work, as well as going home for their lunchbreak. At the exit, cyclists were seen waiting and ready behind the shipyard gates. At the appointed time, the gates swung open and disgorged cyclists en masse in one whole block onto the roads. This immediately slowed down all other road traffic; including the many workers' specials buses.

Shipyard workers coming towards the town hall on the High Level Bridge in 1957; the Vickers engineering sheds are in the background and the Coffee House is in the distance behind the second PD2. Meanwhile the first PD2 in view threads its way to Hawcoat.

Virtually all the fleet was required to run the workers' specials at peak times, when they carried around 5,000 people, and even more when it was wet and the bicycles stayed at home. Many of these workers' services turned short and did not cover the whole route. A maximum of 34 buses were required for non-peak operations, (from around 0800 to 1700 hours), with a slight increase for lunchtime, but up to 30 buses more could be needed for workers' specials in the morning and evening peaks.

Looking across to the High Level Bridge from the dockyard area on Michaelson Road, the dockyard traffic is heading towards the town hall, which can be seen in the middle. This 1951 photo has also captured one of the four 1933 TS4 single-deckers that up to 1950 were on the Oxford Street to Risedale service. It became double-decker operated in 1950 and was extended from Oxford Street to the new housing estate at Ormsgill. In 1953 it was then extended at the Risedale end to Newbarns, the new housing estate. The TS4s were to be withdrawn between 1951 and 1955. One became a mobile clinic and another, a mobile library.

As was noted in the bus timetable: "at the morning, lunchtime and evening peak periods, additional services will operate between the various termini and Vickers-Armstrong works." Ominously, the timetable also mentioned, "services operated especially for Workpeople are liable to suspension if not needed".

Besides the main shipyard workers' specials for Vickers, there were also timetabled workers' services to the Lister's textile factory at Roose, the ironworks, the hoopworks, the cellophane factory and to the central railway station.

The main town terminus for all but one Barrow Corporation route was around the town hall, with the other terminus being at nearby Ramsden Square for the Barrow joint route to Ulverston with Ribble. Ribble also had other services from Barrow.

A front offside view of buses on Bridge Road in the dockyard area. The first one is for St. James, on Blake Street; a short working on the Cemetery route.

At peak periods most of the mainland services (those to Ormsgill, Cemetery, Hawcoat, Harrell Lane and Newbarns) were extended back half a mile from the town hall area over the High Level Bridge on Michaelson Road and into the shipyard area on Barrow Island. The exception to these extended shipyard starts, was the Ulverston via Coast Road route, which whilst it had timetabled workers short running services to Roa Island and to Bardsea, none of these were shown in the 1961 timetable as being extended from the town hall to Vickers.

Meanwhile, the Tea House service to Roose already terminated near to the shipyard on Barrow Island. Also, the three routes out to Walney Island already passed the shipyard in normal service, so the workers' specials continued straight from there. Finally, the Ulverston via Dalton route was extended from Ramsden Square to the Coffee House; this being near to Vickers on Michaelson Road on Barrow Island.

Barrow Town Hall with Leyland/Park Royal buses on the left and on the right, a Crossley.

The routes operated in 1961 were:

From	To	Blind Colour	Journey Time	Headway in Minutes
Abbey	Biggar Bank	Green	23 minutes	7.5 to 15
Cemetery	North Scale		23 minutes	15
Hawcoat	Newbarns	Red	24 minutes	10 to 15
Ormsgill *	Harrel Lane	Yellow	34 minutes	7.5 to 15
Rainey Park *	Harrel Lane	Yellow	25 minutes	7.5 to 15
Roose	Town Hall	Blue	19 minutes	7.5 to 15
Barrow +	Dalton and Ulverston		28 minutes	10
Barrow	Coast Road and Ulverston		51/53 minutes	1 to 2 hourly

* Operated as a Harrel Lane circular, e.g. Ormsgill – Town Hall – Friars Lane – Harrel Lane – Abbey Road – Town Hall – Rainey Park and return, e.g. Rainey Park – Town Hall – Abbey Road – Harrel Lane – Friars Lane – Town Hall – Ormsgill.

+ Joint with Ribble 75% Barrow 25%.

With a classic 1961 Barrow background, Barrow bus 53 on Duke Street looks like it has run in from the Ulverston Coast road route.

Barrow unusually had varied colours for the destination blinds. These had been introduced in 1934, and those being used in 1961 were:

- green background with white letters,
- red background with white letters,
- yellow background with black letters/or yellow background with white letters
- blue background with white letters,
- where no colours were used, then normal, white on black screens were used

I am 99% confident that Barrow had the most comprehensive coloured final destination blinds in the country, and whilst Bournemouth also used coloured blinds (blue, red, green and orange) these were on the via screens. Barrow continued with them until the last of the post-war Leylands were withdrawn. It has also been reported the practice started again in February 1990 but was phased out in 1993.

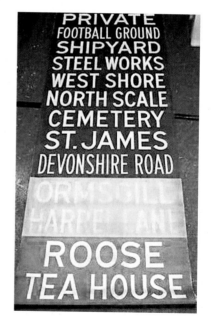

Coloured destination blinds show the former "red" route from Hawcoat to The Shore that was changed to go to Newbarns, and The Shore became Rainey Park on the Ormsgill / Harrel Lane Circular routes.

The development of these routes had been:

April 1932: Conversion to bus routes from trams

- Abbey to Town Hall to Biggar Bank (Green blinds)
- Roose to Town Hall to Tea House (Blue)
- Hawcoat to Town Hall to The Shore (Red)
- Ormsgill to Town Hall to Harrel Lane (Yellow)
- Cemetery to Town Hall to North Scale (Black)

1936

- New: Oxford Street (Victoria Park Hotel) to Town Hall to Risedale; this was operated by single-deckers.

11th April 1950

- New: Oxford Street to Town Hall to Friars Lane to Harrell Lane to Oxford Street and this replaced: Oxford Street to Town Hall to Risedale.
- New: Ormsgill to Town Hall to Risedale was now operated by double-deckers and had replaced: Ormsgill to Town Hall to Harrel Lane.

1st February 1953

- Risedale was extended to Newbarns.

29th May 1955

- New: Hawcoat to Town Hall to Newbarns, replacing the route previously starting in Ormsgill and it also replaced: Hawcoat – The Shore.
- New: Ormsgill – Town Hall – Friars Lane – Harrel Lane – Abbey Road – Town Hall – The Shore and return; this replaced: Oxford Street to Town Hall to Friars Lane to Harrell Lane to Oxford Street.

April 1957

- The Shore was changed to Rainey Park (a new housing estate).

12th November 1959

- Alternate termini at Roose, either the Ship Inn or North Row. Reportedly the North Row option was cancelled in 1964.

Meanwhile a full top destination blind in the late 1950s contained the following destinations **(with the main terminus highlighted):**

- Town Hall, Private, Football Ground, Shipyard, Steelworks, Docks, St. Aloysius.
- White House (this was passed by the Abbey and Harrel Lane routes).
- Washington (passed by on the routes to Roose and Harrel Lane).
- West Shore, **North Scale**, St. James, **Cemetery**.
- Devonshire Road, **Ormsgill**, Friars Lane, **Harrell Lane**, The Shore, Southampton Street, Promenade, **Rainey Park**.
- **Roose, Ship Inn, Tea House**.
- **Biggar Bank**, Amphitrite Street, Black Butts Lane, **Abbey**.
- **Hawcoat**, Hawcoat Lane, Oxford Street, Risedale Road, **Newbarns**.
- **Barrow, Dalton, Swarthmoor, Ulverston**, Rampside, Roa Island, Goadsbarrow, Baycliffe, Bardsea. These last five were all on the Ulverston Coast Road route.

The lower front via blinds were the normal white on black and for the record a full via blind listing in the late 1950s was:

Teesdale Road (North Scale route), Blake Street (Cemetery route), Devonshire Road (Ormsgill route), Town Centre, Farm Street (Tea House route), Dalton (Ulverston direct), Roa Island, Coast Road (both Ulverston), Abbey Road (principally Harrel Lane), Abbey (Ulverston route), Ship Inn (Roose route), Holker Street (Cemetery route), Ramsden Street (Harrel Lane and Roose routes), Greengate Street (Newbarns route), Circular (Harrel Lane) and Cellophane (a workers' special). The last two did not show the word "via" on the actual blind.

Ribble buses in Barrow

Beside the Corporation buses, Ribble buses were found in Barrow. These turned at Ramsden Square from where the following routes ran mainly along Abbey Road to the following places:

Route	Destinations	Journey Time	Main Headway	Comments
517	Ambleside via Dalton, Ulverston, Newby Bridge, Bellman Ground, Bowness, Windermere.	1 hour 44 minutes	Every 2 hours (odd hours).	517, 520 and 533 were shown as being jointly operated with Barrow CT. However, I never saw any Barrow buses operating these routes.
520 *	As 517 to Ambleside, but via Storrs Hall instead of Bellman Ground.	1 hour 49 minutes	Every 2 hours.	
526 / 527	Ulverston via Great Urswick, Scales and Beckside (526) or Great Urswick (527). Although all the other routes left Barrow via Abbey Road, these left on Hindpool Road (the parallel road to Duke Street) on their way to Roose for Great Urswick.	526 = 45 minutes 527 = 40 minutes	Mainly ran every hour.	These were village routes that ran south of the main 534 route on the A590 and north of the Barrow CT Coast Road route to Ulverston.
533	Kendal via Dalton, Ulverston, Newby Bridge, Cartmel, Grange, Levens.	2 hours 17 minutes	Every 2 hours (even hours).	Six through buses a day, other times ran Newby Bridge to Grange only with connections from the 517 at Newby Bridge.
534	Ulverston via Dalton	28 minutes	Every 10 minutes.	Joint with Barrow on a 75% Ribble and 25% Barrow share.

* Most 520 departures were from Ulverston although it was advertised as a through route, but there was only one timetabled, the last bus from Barrow at 2135 hours. At other times, a change was required off the 534 from Barrow at Ulverston.

Ribble's nearest depot was in Ulverston and single-deckers were used on routes 517/520, 526/527 and 533. Whilst memory fades and I never logged them, I suspect the following batches of buses were being used in 1961:

Ribble had thirty DRN registered Leyland integral Olympics with Weymann B44F bodies new in 1951. In 1961 all of these were allocated in the Lake District at Ambleside, Kendal and Ulverston. They were withdrawn by 1968.

ECK/ERN registered Leyland Royal Tiger PSU1/13s with Leyland B44F bodies with 371 waiting in Ambleside for Barrow. Ribble had 110 of these box looking shallowed roof buses from 1952 and in 1958 they were some of the first Ribble one person operated buses. All had been withdrawn by 1967.

The fifty ERN/FCK registered Leyland Tiger Cub PSUC1/1s with Saunders Roe (Saro) B44F bodies were good looking buses with a distinctive rounded shape. New in 1954 some of them lasted up to 1969 and this one is seen in Lancaster.

For the 534 route, Ribble used their Leyland PD2s double-deckers and again I never logged them, but I expect they were from the following batches of buses:

Ribble had thirty rear doored ECK registered PD2/12 registered Leyland L53RD numbered 1351 to 1380. New in 1952 they went relatively quickly in 1966/1967.

Twenty five HCK/HRN Leyland PD2/13s came next in 1955 with MCCW H61RD bodies and these were numbered 1381 to 1405. 1399 is in Lancaster and like many of the batch, was later used as a training bus.

Barrow's share on the 534 were usually selected from the four Barrow double-deckers with doors (159/160, 147/148) where on the maximum headway, Ribble provided six buses and Barrow two.

Ribble got forty JCK registered PD2/12s with Burlingham H61RD bodies in 1955/1956 numbered 1431 to 1470. Seen on Abbey Road approaching Ramsden Square is 1452.

Barrow's post-war fleet to 1961

In 1961 Barrow Corporation Transport had a relatively standard fleet of navy blue and cream Leylands. Sixty were double-decker Leyland PD2s that had entered service with Park Royal bodies, and three were single-deckers. With between 26 and 34 buses required for the normal timetabled services, the balance from the fleet were used for workers' specials and as cover for maintenance.

The PD2s came in batches, by registration, of twelve and eighteen in 1949; ten in 1950, ten in 1951 and ten in 1958. The fifty-vehicle batching on the 1949 and 1950 deliveries was partly inconsistent as some buses from the 18 x 1949 batch and the ten from 1950, have chassis numbers that are not aligned with the registration batch sequencing.

The first fifty, from 1949 to 1951, were numbered from 111 to 160 and had replaced Leyland 38 TDs new in 1938 to 1942 and eleven utility Daimlers and Guys from 1942/1943. They all had almost identical 5 bay bodies by Park Royal with 111 to 150 being of composite construction and 151 to 160 being metal-framed. Barrow was very quick to replace its pre-war and wartime fleet of buses and in so doing it also gained a large fleet of the recently allowed 8 foot wide buses. However, the 5 bay body was essentially what had been the pre-war norm.

There were also some small detail differences in some of the batches and the whole 50 buses were also very similar to the smaller fleet of AEC Regents/4 bay Park Royals supplied to Morecambe.

In 1958 came PD2s 161 to 170 with a different style of 4 bay body from Park Royal and these had replaced twenty Crossleys from 1948.

117 when new at Park Royal in 1949. The via blind of Farm Street was on the route to the Tea House. Like all of Park Royal bodied 111 to 150 they were of composite construction.

For comparison here is Morecambe 69, an AEC Regent built in 1950 with Park Royal 4-bay H33/26R bodywork. The rear was the same as used on pre-war bodies.

The Crossley's 40 to 49 and 101 to 110

Crossley 42 was new in May 1948 on the Ulverston via Dalton service. Withdrawn in 1956 and with three others it saw further use with Beeline Roadways in West Hartlepool.

The first batch of wide Crossleys were delivered in early 1948 and all but one went in 1956. The others came later in 1948, lasted until 1958/1959 and were then replaced in 1958 by Leylands, numbered 161 to 170. One batch of the Crossleys had interior red seating with "MCTD" match strikers on the upper deck, Manchester Corporation taking delivery of Crossleys at the same time.

107 came in November 1948 and is parked on spare ground behind the town hall. Craven House is now built near there and this building fronts on Michaelson Road.

Leylands 111 to 122

120 makes its way across Michaelson Bridge from North Scale on its way to Cemetery.

In late 1961, Leylands 111 to 120 were sold to Merthyr Tydfil Corporation where they stayed until 1966 to 1968; the remaining two, 121/122, were used until 1966 as driver trainers. The replacements were Leyland/Massey front entrance buses numbered 1 to 10, re-numbered 101 to 110 in 1970.

121 is parked in the Hindpool Road Depot and was destined to become a trainer bus from 1964 to 1966.

Leylands 123 to 140

126 on Church Street at the junction of Greengate Street. The Welcome Inn (later renamed the Sheffield) is on the left, and Pickford's is on the right. 126 is working the 29th May 1955 route to Hawcoat from Newbarns, that formerly had started in Ormsgill.

Leylands 141 to 150

This 1950 batch was rebodied by Roe in 1959. The reasons for rebodying have been debated. Some say this was due to composite construction with timber deterioration (however, this seems strange, as all of 111 to 150 had the same composite bodies, yet, only 141 to 150 were rebodied). Others have said, and this seems more likely, rebodying was due to large recertification requirements, as all of 111 to 160 had entered service closely together.

Photographic evidence would seem to indicate the Park Royal window frames were re-used by Roe, as they retained the identical Park Royal lower 5 bay format, whereas other new Roe bodies at the time were using a 4-bay design. The cab, rear and front were, however, classic Roe.

148 before rebodying and near to the town hall, ready for a short to Baycliffe on the Coast Road service. Un-timetabled in the summer 1961 timetable it was a 38-minute run and only 10 minutes short of Ulverston.

150 in August 1959 at Roe showing they that were delivered mainly unpainted. It was said Barrow removed the original bodies and broke them up, with only the chassis coming to Roe, also that the bodies from 143/149/150 were reported sold for scrap in May 1959. Others, however, say some Park Royal parts were kept and sent over to Roe.

149 with its later 1959 Roe body; it makes a good comparison with Park Royal bodied 148, page 24.

149 with Roe body waits to leave the town centre for Newbarns.

147 shows the rear doors that it shared with 148. It is in the updated 1962 livery that originally used a more yellow coloured cream livery; this would soon fade and so was replaced by the lighter/paler cream.

Leylands 151 to 160

This batch of metal framed 5 bay Park Royal buses were easily recognisable by the upper deck opening front windows.

Leyland 153 at Park Royal when new. This batch was of metal construction, unlike the previous composite bodies on 111 to 150. The via blind of Blake St was used on the Cemetery route but normally "Town Hall" was shown instead.

153 in an experimental application with a "very cream" shade.

154 leaving Newbarns with red blinds for Hawcoat and also showing the normal whiter shade of cream.

159 with rear doors in the post-1962 livery. Being so near the coast Barrow had problems with paint fade. Indeed in 1965 they experimented with a brighter blue but as the cream became faded the brighter blue did not match and so a return to royal blue was made.

Leylands 161 to 170

These 1958 buses had a totally different 4 bay body design to the earlier Park Royals; the design was new in 1954. They replaced the remaining Crossleys in 1958/1959.

170, the last of the batch, near to the town hall at the top end of Church Street going past Keay's Chemists.

The Barrow bus allocation pattern in 1961 was normally to use the newer 141 to 170 buses on the Monday to Sunday all day basic headway services, with the older buses numbered 111 to 140, appearing mainly on the extra journeys.

162 in from Roose (Ship Inn) going to the Tea House less than a mile away. It is waiting near the post office on Michaelson Road and will soon head across the High Level Bridge on its short journey.

Morecambe had similar bodied buses as seen on their 79 from 1954 when this design was introduced.

1 to 10 HEO 271-280 Leyland PD2A/27 Massey H64F
(renumbered 101 to 110 in 1970)

Barrow had considered buying further bodies by Park Royal, but at that time, Royal Park was only offering an ugly squared off body, bought for example, by Southampton and said to be based on the Bridgemaster model body.

The Masseys entered service in late 1961; four entered service in September, four in October and the final two in November; Morecambe also bought similar Massey bodies.

The Park Royal Southampton body that Barrow did not want.

Massey 9 waits at Biggar Bank.

Seen after the 1970 renumbering are 106 and 103 behind the town hall. They were the last new double-deckers bought until 1983.

One of Morecambe's Massey bodied PD2s from 1961 is seen here after the takeover/amalgamation by Lancaster CT.

Single Deckers

The three single-deckers always were elusive and were said to be used as one man operated on the very sparsely populated Ulverston Coast Road service. I actually never saw them there when we regularly went to the Coast Road to visit relations in Rampside, Goadsbarrow and Aldingham; in fact, the only place I ever saw them in 1961 was at the 1936 built depot in Hindpool Road.

All Leyland 50 from 1952 (renumbered 65 from 1963) and in a 50/50 livery style is on a short to Roa Island on the Ulverston via Coast Road route; it was withdrawn in 1966 when the Strachan-bodied single-deckers numbered 50 to 54 entered service.

Barrow Royal Tiger 52 (and later 66 in 1963) in the original livery. New in 1955 with Massey body, in 1957 it received dual purpose seats (as seen here) and was then reseated back to bus seats in 1967. It was withdrawn in 1974.

Sometime between 1963 and 1967 we see 53 (now 67 from 1963) at the front and in the "yellowy" cream with a single blue waistband livery. 52 (66 from 1963) in the background is still in the pre-1962 livery but now has the 50/50 livery; it is also undergoing lower front repairs and has also by now gained a driver's door. Double-decker in the middle 129 was withdrawn in 1967.

Developments from 1962 to 1989

Route changes took place as follows:

9th February 1963: Cemetery to North Scale was extended to West Shore but this extension was cut back on 29th May 1966 and extended at the other end from Cemetery to Dane Avenue, so it then became Dane Avenue-Cemetery-Town Hall-North Scale.

29th May 1966: West Shore was now served by an extension from Rainey Park.

28th March 1971: Coast Road route goes via Bardsea village.

7th August 1973: Dane Avenue was extended to Hawcoat Estate for a year's trial, which was confirmed on 9th September 1974 when the former Lakes Parade termini was extended 0.36 miles to Ravenglass Road.

8th August 1976: Roose Ship Inn was extended 0.70 miles to the Holbeck Park Estate (the terminus was called Holbeck Farm).

The main development in this period was the start of one person operations (OPO) that directly affected the fleet policy, so single-deckers were needed from the early 1960s. Whilst OPO had started on the 6th October 1958 on the Coast Road route to Ulverston using buses 50/52 (and later 53), developments proceeded rapidly from 1963. The phased conversion to OPO, coupled with new single-deckers, also paralleled the withdrawal of the early Leyland PD2s.

The OPO introductions and the buses that made such conversions possible, are:

28th April 1963 Cemetery to North Scale, using new buses numbered 68 to 73; these replaced some of the PD2s from the 123 to 140 batch.

1963 Leyland Leopards 68 to 73 had boxy looking East Lancashire bodies. Barrow stayed with the Leyland Leopard/East Lancs combination from 1963 to 1969 apart from in 1966.

72 in Hindpool Road Depot yard; at least the rear end had a curved roof. This 1963 batch had a long life, being withdrawn in 1983 when they were replaced by three brand new double-deckers numbered 104 to 106.

The next conversion was on 13th August 1967 when Roose to Tea House went OPO. 50 to 54 had been delivered in 1966, when they replaced more of the PD2s from the 123 to 140 batch and also single-decker 65 (formerly 50).

53 from the batch 50 to 54 were delivered in 1966. They were Leyland Leopards with Strachan's B51D bodies. The bodies had to be rebuilt in 1974/1975, this remedial work being undertaken by Barrow's normal bodybuilder, East Lancs. This work involved strengthening the front, rear and the rear bays. They were withdrawn ten years later and replaced by one new and two ex-London double-deckers, numbered 107 to 109.

50 showing its rebuilt/new rear end that replaced the larger former BET window style.

On 6th October 1968 Newbarns to Hawcoat was converted to OPO with buses 55 to 65 that were new in 1967/1968. These also had replaced more PD2s from the 123 to 140 batch.

The 1967 batch (55 to 59) of Leopards had bodies built by the East Lancs subsidiary Neepsend. 57 is in the depot with the nearside rear of the earlier 68 to 73 batch, in the right background.

62 is from the 1968 East Lancs built batch numbered 60 to 64. All of 55 to 64 were to pass over to Barrow Borough Transport (BBT) in 1986.

The next OPO conversion was on 4th January 1970, Abbey to Biggar Bank and also, on the same date, the Dane Avenue to North Scale route was converted to OPO. These conversions were enabled by buses 55 to 64 from 1967/1968 and also by 45 to 49 new in 1969. These fifteen buses had replaced the last of the 123 to 140 batch and also all of the 151 to 160 batch; the last Leyland non rebodied Park Royals.

46, from the 1969 batch number 45 to 49 batch, passes by some camera-watching passengers.

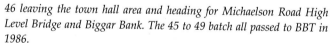

46 leaving the town hall area and heading for Michaelson Road High Level Bridge and Biggar Bank. The 45 to 49 batch all passed to BBT in 1986.

25th September 1971 and the last route to become OPO was Ulverston via Dalton and enabled by buses 1 to 5 new in 1971; these replaced some of the Roe rebodied Leyland PD2s. 1 to 5 had low floor Daimler SRG chassis with rear Gardner engines.

More East Lancs bodies were on the 1 to 5 batch and in Hindpool Road Depot is 2. These had a lower front position for easier access and the wider entrance doors had also replaced the former preference for dual doored buses. Their "front drooping nose look" is clearly shown. All five went over to BBT in 1986.

After the completion of OPO with single-deckers, normal fleet replacement continued with further single-deckers from 1974 to 1980. After this there was a return to double-deckers until the end of BCT and the birth in 1986 of BBT.

The single-deckers bought from 1974 to 1978, were twelve Cumbrian built Leyland Nationals. These came in three batches numbered 6 to 10, 11 to 15, and 16 to 17. These saw off the last of the Roe-bodied PD2s and the 1958 Leyland PD2s leaving only the 1961 Massey-bodied Leylands double-deckers. With a brief interlude of two strange buses from Dennis in 1979 and four more Leyland National 2s in 1980, these effectively ended the Leyland PD2 era in 1981 when 109/110 (originally 9, 10) were the last to be withdrawn. However, double-deckers were to return in late 1982.

11 from 1977 is typical of the Leyland Nationals bought from 1974 to 1978.

18 and 19 were East Lancs bodied Dennis Dominators with Gardner engines and in this first view arguably tidier looking than the earlier Daimlers 1 to 5. Here Dominator 18 has left the Tea House termini and is crossing over Bridge Road for Michaelson Road and the High Level Bridge towards Town Hall for Roose.

This image of 18 demonstrates the "other side" of the East Lancs body, where the cover for the engine looks to be "an added extra". It makes little attempt to blend in with the rest of the body as was done with the earlier Daimlers 1 to 5.

Leyland National 2 numbered 22 from 1980 on Abbey Road.

Double-deckers returned when in 1982 and 1984 BCT bought five ex-London Transport DMS class Leyland Fleetlines that were new in 1976/1977. These were originally dual doored but were converted by the dealers Ensign to front entrance only. Barrow numbered the ones bought in December 1982 101 to 103, followed in 1984 by 108/109.

An offside view of 108 at Ormsgill Terminus accompanied by three dogs. 108 demonstrates the retention of the central staircase on this former dual doored bus.

New double-deckers came in 1983 with 104 to 106 followed by 107 in 1984. These were Leyland Atlanteans with well-proportioned NCME bodies. 107 is seen waiting at the West Shore extension to the Rainey Park route on the Harrel Lane circular.

The End of Barrow Corporation Transport

In 1986 Bus Deregulation was enacted, so a commercially formed company was separated out from the previous Corporation ownership, and Barrow Borough Transport (BBT) took over the bus operations.

Barrow had to register services they intended operating for the 26th October, and these included:

Daily

- Harrell Lane to West Shore
- Ormsgill to Newbarns
- Biggar Bank to Hawcoat (Lakes Parade)
- Ormsgill to Harrel Lane

Day time routes (every 10 minutes)

- Biggar Bank to Dalton
- Hawcoat (Lake Parade) to Newbarns
- Hawcoat (Ravenglass Avenue) to North Scale
- Roose (Holbeck Farm) to Tea House

Evening routes (every 20 minutes)

- Roose (Holbeck Farm) to North Scale
- Newbarns to West Shore

Deregulation also meant that any company could now basically run anywhere and neighbours Ribble, part of the large National Bus Company, was quick off the blocks and started operating services in Barrow with Mercedes minibuses on the following main routes, and only on a Monday to Saturday:

- Ocean Road, Walney to Ormsgill
- Newbarns to Furness Hospital (Hawcoat)

They also registered for Monday to Friday operation from Town Centre to North Scale and they won a tender for a Sunday service, from Roose to North Scale. The battle lines had been drawn. Ribble offered high frequency services branded as "Minilink", and unlike Barrow who stayed mainly on the main roads as they had always done, the Ribble buses went into the estates with a hail and ride system. Barrow started to lose traffic.

For those routes not served by commercial operations, a tendering process was used on, for example, early morning and Sunday journeys. Ribble won all of these. Additionally, under the tender process, Barrow also lost to Ribble both of the Ulverston routes.

BBT had two reactions: the first was to shed buses, so they reduced the fleet by ten, whilst bringing in six new Dodge minibuses in 1986 to compete with Ribble on the town routes. These six were later followed, in 1988, with seventeen Talbot low floor minibuses and also three more second-hand double-deckers in 1989. Ribble in turn also brought in similar Talbot minibuses.

The second reaction by BBT was in November 1987, when they started to start a new service from Barrow to Kendal, along with two Kendal town services. The Kendal town routes were joint with the former Lancaster Corporation and were solely intended by Barrow and Lancaster as a retaliation against Ribble. However, Barrow soon withdrew in February 1988 as they were now seriously losing out at home as Ribble continued to refine the route network there. Lancaster stayed on in Kendal until September 1989.

Meanwhile in March 1988, Ribble had a management buyout and arguably then became even more competitive. At the same time in Barrow, after a policy disagreement, a senior manager left, followed by the managing director who resigned due to ill-health. Reported losses since deregulation were almost £1 million. and consequently, administrators were appointed in December 1988.

1989 was to be a decisive year. First Ribble were taken over by the fast-growing Stagecoach bus company on 21st April, then on 26th May Barrow Borough Transport ceased to trade and buses were withdrawn at two hours' notice. Ribble took over operations, the depot at Hindpool Road and also 24 buses that were transferred away so that the six blue Dodge minibuses, eleven Leyland Nationals and seven double-deckers were not seen on the Barrow streets. Next, on the 18th June, Stagecoach Cumberland took over all operations in Barrow and surrounding districts and they are still there today.

Other developments

The bus depot in Hindpool Road was severely damaged in the winter of 1994/1995 and was eventually sold. Stagecoach transferred its depot to R Brady's and Sons Limited yard on Walney Road on 23rd/24th April.

In 2012 the Stagecoach fleet at Barrow was nineteen single-deckers and fifteen double-deckers and was still operating a successful high frequency network.

Changing work patterns and lifestyles, the growth of TV and car travel all contributed away from the 60 plus double decker fleet of the 1950s. The changed legislation in the 1980s meant the former municipal owned companies had to become totally commercial minded. Barrow simply could not compete in this new arena; therefore, eventually like so many others, they "left the stage".

Fleet lists can be provided upon request to enquiries@stenlake.co.uk